INSIGHT HERITAGE

THE PRISON EXPERIENCE
AT THE INQUISITOR'S PALACE
Vittoriosa

KENNETH GAMBIN

PHOTOGRAPHY
DANIEL CILIA

HERITAGE BOOKS
IN ASSOCIATION WITH
H Heritage Malta
2004

HOW TO GET TO THE INQUISITOR'S PALACE

By bus:
Bus nos 1, 2, 4, 6 from Valletta main bus terminus and stop at Vittoriosa bus terminus.

By car:
Main roads leading to the Three Cities and then follow the road signs to Vittoriosa and the Inquisitor's Palace.

The Inquisitor's Palace
Main Gate Str
Vittoriosa CSP 02
Malta
Tel: 2166 3731,
    2182 7006
info@heritagemalta.org

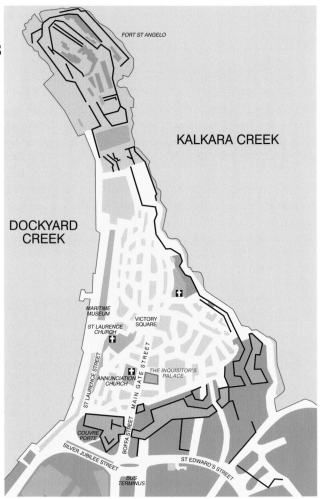

Insight Heritage Guides Series No: 8
General Editor: Louis J. Scerri

Published by Heritage Books, a subsidiary of Midsea Books Ltd, Carmelites Street, Sta Venera HMR 11, Malta
sales@midseabooks.com

Insight Heritage Guides is a series of books intended to give an insight into aspects and sites of Malta's rich heritage, culture and traditions.

Produced by Mizzi Design & Graphic Services
Printed by Gutenberg Press

Editorial © Heritage Books
Literary © Kenneth Gambin
Photography © Daniel Cilia

First published 2004

ISBN: 99932-7-000-8

FOREWORD

The Inquisitor's Palace, sited in the heart of the historical city of Vittoriosa, is one of the very few surviving palaces of its kind which could be found scattered all over Europe and South America in the early modern period. Fortunately, Malta's Inquisitor's Palace has always hosted high-ranking officials representing the main powers on the island throughout its five centuries of history, and this ensured its survival. Although much has been changed in its structure, the palace remains a gem, a representative of the tumultuous history and European cultural heritage of the Maltese islands. It also contains one of the rare early modern prison structures which still survives and which reflects a particular imprisonment philosophy.

Unfortunately, not much attention has been devoted to the history of the building. The same applies to the prisons of the palace, the methods of imprisonment, and the treatment of inmates by the Holy Office. It is indeed often difficult to separate fact from fiction. Fortunately the incredibly rich archives of the Inquisition held in the Cathedral Museum of Mdina makes possible the detailed reconstruction of what really went on inside the prisons. The following is a revised edition of the first systematic but humble attempt at doing away with the many myths and legends that have arisen concerning the Inquisition tribunal. It will also hopefully help shed some more light on the history of the Inquisitor's Palace in general.

This publication also makes an integral part of Heritage Malta's efforts at increasing interpretation facilities in all its museums and sites, thus rendering them more accessible and enriching the visitor's experience.

Kenneth Gambin
Curator - Inquisitor's Palace

List of abbreviations

AIM	**Archives of the Inquisition of Malta**
BAV	**Bibliotheca Apostolica Vaticana**
Chigi	**Archivio Chigi**
Corr.	**Corrispondenza**
f./ff.	**folio/folios**
Proc. Civ.	**Processi Civili**
Proc. Crim.	**Processi Criminali**

INTRODUCTION

Imprisonment is the imposition of involuntary bodily confinement of people convicted of criminal offences; it forms part of a wider category of physical punishments that restrict the individual's freedom of movement. Incarceration also provides a means of punishment which offers the authorities control over the offender without necessarily abusing his body.

However, the emergence of the prison as the chief institution for combating crime and dealing with offenders is relatively new. It emerged barely 200 years ago, towards the end of the early modern period, amid sceptical comments about its efficacy.[1] Michel Foucault interprets it as part of

a wider attempt by bourgeois society to discipline, dominate, and punish the slightest deviation from 'proper behaviour'.[2] Until then those imprisoned were merely 'birds of passage'. Prisons had a preventive, not a punitive function,[3] and were reserved mainly for those awaiting trial, with the actual punishment being carried out publicly in the form of severe corporal suffering: execution on the scaffold, mutilation, whipping, or branding in order to 'educate' the spectators.[4]

However, social forces brought about a 'culture change'. One of the most important was the influence of Canon Law, with its emphasis not only on the vindictive aspect of prisons, but also their use as instruments towards the re-education and rehabilitation of the prisoners, especially in the Papal States. As a direct consequence, more importance started being given to more humane prison conditions.[5]

Moreover, by the late eighteenth century there developed a marked tendency towards non-physical and private discipline. These developments reflected wider changing social attitudes towards offenders as well as the human body. The triumph of incarceration as a form of punishment was the result of a growing sensitivity to violence and an aversion to physical suffering, which left their impact on what was deemed acceptable forms of punishment, especially by the higher echelons of society.[6] And the Inquisition, with its emphasis on imprisonment, was one of the mainstays of what has been described as 'the most conspicuous change in the long-term evolution of the penal system'.[7]

Opposite: **Interior of one of the communal prison cells**

The main facade of the Inquisitor's Palace

THE INQUISITION

The coat-of-arms of the Roman Inquisition

The Roman Inquisition, better known as the Holy Office, was the first official stand by the Catholic Church against Luther's Protestant Reformation of 1517. It was established in 1542 by Pope Paul III by means of the bull *Licet ab Initio*. The era of theological uncertainties was over. A strong reaction developed, reemphasizing Catholic dogma and reasserting the liturgical ceremonies of the Church, whose hierarchy was further centralized in order to be in a sounder offensive position. The Inquisition was on the front line of attack in this programme which indeed constituted its *raison d'être*: 'to inculcate a sense of correct behaviour and the correct beliefs expected from a Christian' as established by the official decrees of the Council of Trent (1545-63), thus reforming the religious culture of the masses.[8] It subordinated all aspects of life and government to an overarching ideology, a grand design, and acted as a watchdog against all kinds of heretical practices, including blasphemy, apostasy to Islam, bigamy, perusing of prohibited books, and a myriad of magical beliefs.

The Roman Inquisition was officially set up in Malta in 1574. One could either be denounced or else choose to appear spontaneously in front of the inquisitor to confess and admit guilt. Torture, which could not last longer than thirty minutes, was used rarely, and was mild when compared to that used by contemporary secular governments. The accused would have his hands tied behind his back with a rope attached to a pulley in the ceiling. He would then be pulled up in the air and let down for a number of times. The absolute majority of the sentences, especially for first-time offenders, were of a spiritual nature, including fasting and prayer. Recidivists, however, could face public beatings, rowing on the galleys of the Order of St John, exile, or imprisonment.

Secrecy was the basic rule on which the entire inquisitorial system was based. Inquisitors and their ministers were bound by very strict oaths of secrecy. If these were not respected, they would incur an excommunication which only the cardinal inquisitors of the Holy Congregation of Rome could remove. One of the immediate consequences of this precept was the birth of a particularly secure prison system in which to lock up the accused and isolate them from contact with the outside world. Not observing this rule would have meant the potential collapse of the whole structure of the Inquisition. In reality, however, as a reflection of contemporary attitudes to imprisonment, the availability of adequate prisons was one of the principal problems for the day-to-day proper functioning and administration of Inquisition tribunals across Europe in the early modern period. The Maltese Holy Office was no exception.

PRISON STRUCTURE

Like so many other tribunals of the Inquisition, the inadequacy of the prison cells constituted one of the major problems of the Vittoriosa Palace from 1574 onwards, the very year when it started being used as the official residence of the inquisitors and apostolic delegates of Malta.[9]

Not having been constructed with the specific intention to be used by the Inquisition, the Birgu palace far from respected the official conditions of a prison as laid down in theoretical treatises on architecture. According to eminent architects such as Leon Battista Alberti and Andrea Palladio, a prison had to be built in a specific and safe topographic context, surrounded by a thick wall with a number of watch-out towers. Its main door had to be very strong, capable of withstanding a crowd assault and

prisoners had to be separated according to age, sex, and social condition. In reality, however, such suggestions had little practical effect upon the reality of contemporary prison building. Distinctive prison architecture and a specific philosophy of treatment did not start to be put in practice before the eighteenth century.[10] Only the *Carceri Nuove* (1650s) and the *Casa di Rieducazione* (1703), both in Rome, approached somewhat the above-mentioned specifications.[11] The rest of the prisons throughout Europe were still a far cry from all theoretical guidelines.

In the late sixteenth century, the palace still did not have a prison complex composed of a cluster of cells. Probably, however, there were some rooms that had already been used as cells before, since the building

A communal prison cell

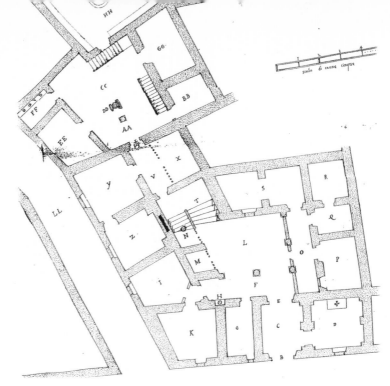

Ground floor plan of the palace c. 1600. Letters I, P, Q, R, S, EE and GG were used as prison cells

had been used as the seat of the *Magna Curia Castellania*, that is the civil law courts of the Order of St John. In 1574, when Mgr. Pietro Dusina arrived as the first general inquisitor of the Maltese islands, the palace had been vacant for three years, from when the Order had left Vittoriosa to occupy the new city of Valletta in 1571. In fact one of the very first measures that Dusina took upon his arrival at the palace in Vittoriosa was to repair the prison cells and to fix various door locks.[12] Moreover a number of rooms on the ground and first floor levels had to be converted into emergency prison cells. These rooms were not arranged in any systematic pattern and were probably selected as prisons on the basis of immediate practical considerations. In all, seven ground-floor rooms were reserved for male prisoners, while females had to do with a single room on the main floor. Still there was not enough space for all the prisoners and the rooms lacked the basic facilities to

be used as cells. The complete inadequacy of three of the ground-floor cells emerges from the fact that they were described as *inhabitabili* by the ministers of the tribunal themselves, since they had no light from any window. Moreover, the humidity of some of the cells, especially those situated on the lower level, was the cause of the constant deterioration of the iron bars, wooden doors, locks, and even the walls of the prisons, which needed incessant attention over the years.[13]

The prison issue was not an emergency only in the early years of the tribunal in Malta. Only towards the mid-seventeenth century, following numerous structural interventions by various inquisitors, was a section of the palace successfully cut off from the rest of the building to be used as a prison complex. One of the first interventions occurred in 1605, when Inquisitor Ettore Diotallevi (1605-07) felt the need to repair the prisons. He took the

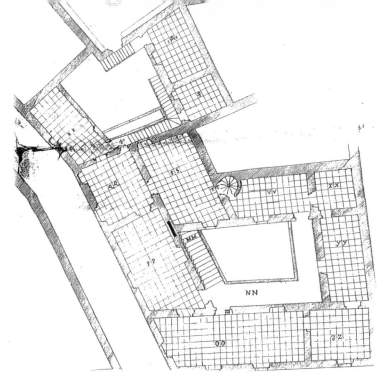

Below and bottom: Iron apparatus for the security of prison doors

initiative and informed the Holy Congregation only after the works that had been undertaken. The latter agreed with the project, but stipulated that in future any expenses had to be communicated to Rome to be approved beforehand.[14] Evidently Diotallevi's repairs had not been carried out satisfactorily in all areas of the prison. Two years later a man was able to dig a hole in the prison wall to the street outside, not to escape, but to let a woman inside during the night.[15]

In 1610 Inquisitor Evangelista Carbonese (1608-14) wrote to the Holy Congregation about the basic need to build new prison cells in a place which was 'more secure and secret'. Rome agreed in principle with Carbonese's plans but he had to find the necessary money to finance the project himself.[16] Since Carbonese had no possibility of obtaining the necessary funds, as a final, desperate, fund-raising measure, he proposed to increase the number of familiars of the Inquisition against payment, so that he could use the money collected to repair the cells. His proposal, however, was turned down, since the Inquisition's policy was not to appear to be after material interests.[17] He had to make the most of the money available at the time.

In 1616 Inquisitor Fabio Della

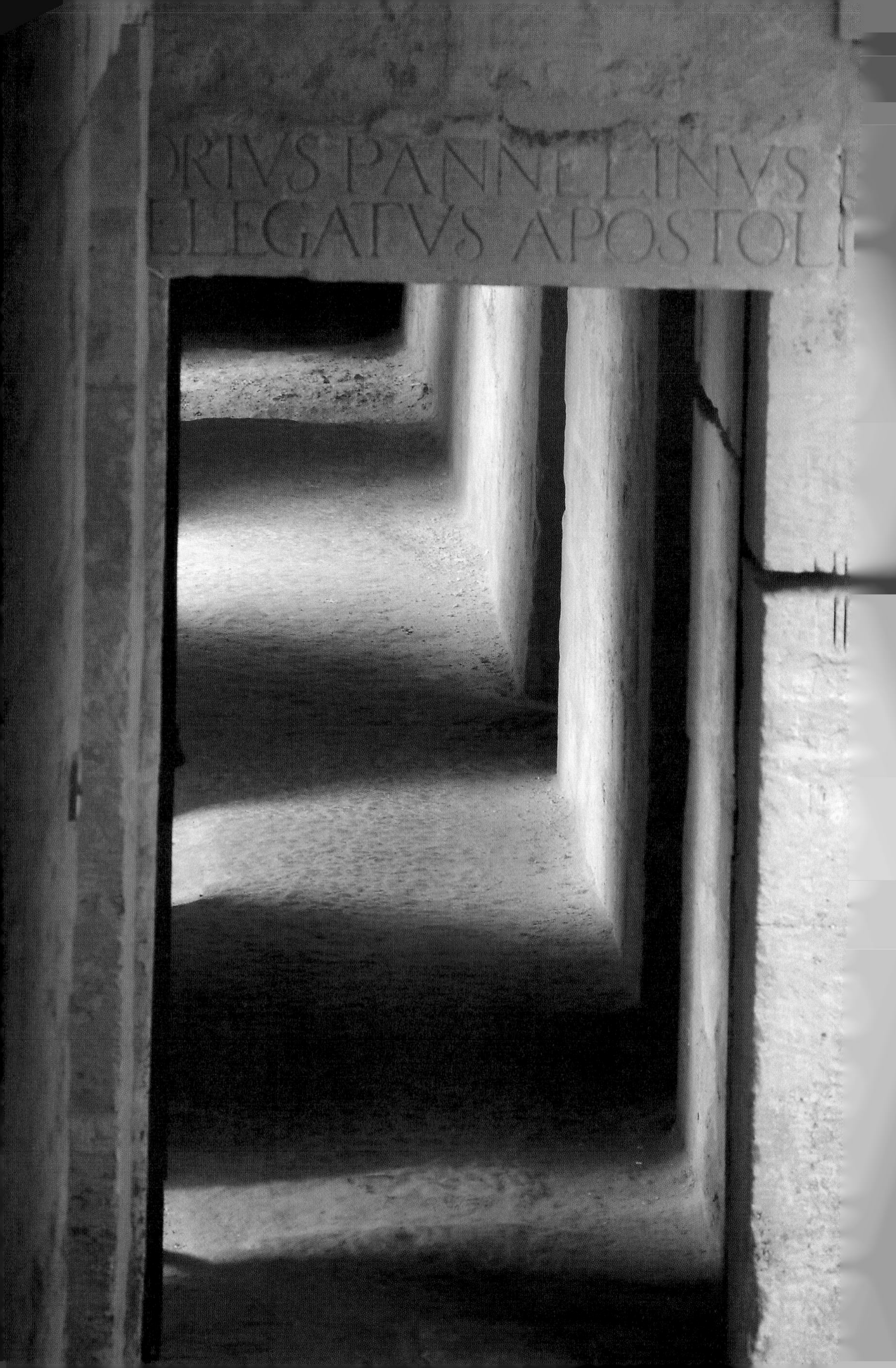
RIUS PANNELINUS
LEGATUS APOSTOL

Lagonessa (1614-19) proposed an ambitious plan for the prisons. He sought and obtained permission to purchase a house which abutted the palace so that a new prison could be built in its place, but the plan did not materialize.[18]

In 1620 permission was given to Inquisitor Antonio Tornielli (1619-21) to refurbish those cells which were in urgent need of attention, but care had to be taken not to overspend because there was not too much money available.[19] Apparently no serious maintenance was carried out because, barely one year later, Inquisitor Paolo Torello (1621-23) was granted permission to strengthen the doors and windows of the cells, the bad condition of which had led to the escape of four prisoners.[20]

The insecurity of the cells was not the only difficulty which inquisitors faced. Lack of space was another problem, and Inquisitor Onorato Visconti (1624-27) panicked during a witch craze in 1625 when he had to arrest forty women accused of sorcery, since the palace was not well equipped enough to host all of them at once.[21]

Problems continued unabated. In the 1630s Inquisitor Fabio Chigi (1634-39, and subsequently Pope Alexander VII, 1655-67) lamented the 'inadequacy of the prison cells … their lack of security and secrecy. No prisoner converts since they all communicate with each other'.[22]

One of the most important developments towards the creation of a proper prison complex took place in the 1640s. Inquisitor Gio. Battista Gori Pannellini (1639-46) purchased the house that abutted the palace on its right flank. In its place he erected seven prison cells, three large ones with high windows on one side

A prison window – most graffiti are found near the window

looking onto the street (*pubbliche*), and four smaller ones facing the garden (*secrete*) on the other side of a central corridor, upon which he constructed his private quarters. The high windows (three metres above floor level), besides capturing as much light as possible from the narrow streets of Vittoriosa, also prevented prisoners from looking out or talking with people outside. The new cells were a very necessary addition to the building, since up till then cells were scattered around the edifice and lacked space and security. Most probably this was the first time that a section of the palace was built with the specific intention to be used as prison cells following a more rational interior plan. The difference in quality was clear also from the outside. Gori Pannellini was particularly happy with the way the cells were being constructed because 'the cells are so strong that the people are frightened and say that it is impossible to escape'.[23] It was his intention, however, that there would be 'more prison cells than prisoners'.[24] The 'secret' cells were meant for those who were serving a prison sentence, while the 'public' cells were used for those

Opposite: The prison section constructed by Gori Pannellini in the 1640s

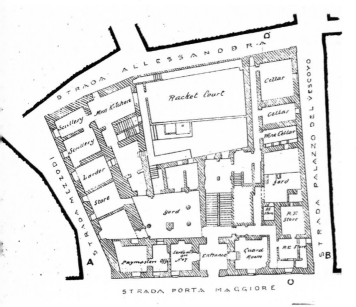

STRADA ALLESSANDOO R·A

Racket Court

Cellar

Cellar

Wine Cellar

Scullery

Mess Kitchen

Sculery

Larder

Store

Yard

Yard

RF Store

RF Store

Paymaster Off

Servant
or
Pay

Entrance

Guard
Room

RE Store

STRADA MEZZODI

STRADA PALAZZO DEL VESCOVO

A

B

STRADA PORTA MAGGIORE

Ground floor plan of the palace as used by the British military forces – prison cells were transformed into cellars and stores

Opposite: **Interior of a prison cell**

under temporary preventive arrest awaiting trial.[25] Each cell was also equipped with a cess-pit for the sanitary requirements of the inmates.

But although Gori Pannellini's project constituted a considerable improvement, not all problems had been solved. The condition of the prison complex was a perennial problem, especially in the 'old' parts of the prisons. For this reason in 1657 Inquisitor Giulio Degli Oddi (1655-58) was advised to reconstruct the prisons in a more appropriate location to avoid two problems which were causing a lot of difficulties to local inquisitors. These were the prisoners' communicating through the flimsy walls with persons outside, and the bad level of hygiene.[26] The restructuring of the cells continued through the tenure of office of Inquisitor Gerolamo Casanate (1658-63), who was ordered to refurbish the cells before imprisoning Sarah Cheevers and Katharine Evans, two British Quakers.[27] But the security of the cells remained apparently

defective since Don Francesco Greg was able to escape in 1659.[28]

Another great improvement towards the security of the palace, especially regarding the possibility of escape, was made in 1659, when after various attempts the palace was finally isolated from all adjoining private property.[29] Notwithstanding these significant efforts, in 1664 Inquisitor Galeazzo Marescotti (1663-66) once again complained about the 'bad situation' of the prisons. He even prepared a plan of how the prisons were in 1664 and of how the new prisons should be constructed.[30] However, no funds were available from Rome for the purpose.[31]

In 1672, in fact, Ferdinando Vassallo and Carlo Vella, procurator and cursor respectively of the Holy Office, testified that there were two sections of the prisons. The first one (built by Gori Pannellini) was described as 'strong and secure', but the other section, (known as Talavera after the owner of the house from whom that part of the palace had been bought), were described as 'rooms', instead of proper cells. Moreover, they were 'built with ordinary Maltese stone, which is very old, and a prisoner can easily escape'. The situation was so serious that when Nicolò Antonio Testaferrata, who was himself employed with the Inquisition as the assistant of the *depositario*, got to know that Don Antonio Muxi, the murderer of his brother Policarpo, was put in the Talavera section, he proposed that he should be transferred to the secular prisons instead.[32] One year later, in 1673, the cells had become so insecure that Inquisitor Ranuccio Pallavicino obtained permission from Rome to change prison sentences to other forms as long as they were less

A plan of 1664 to build a new prison section

Opposite: **Entrance to a solitary cell**

The strong wall leading to the street built by Masserano in 1698

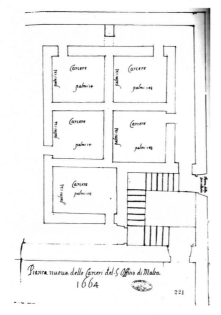

Pianta nuova delle Carceri del S. Offitio di Malta.
1664

221

harsh.[33] It is little wonder that Don Matteo Barlotti[34] and Carlo, a slave of Federico Falson managed to escape from the prisons in 1675 and 1684 respectively.[35] The relatively frequent escapes from the prisons were not a particular characteristic of the Holy Office, however. Even escapes from the prisons of the Order of St John inside Fort St Angelo 'were almost the rule, rather than the exception', and owing to the lax security of the prisons, knights left whenever they liked.[36] This should not come as a surprise since even the central prisons of the Holy Office of Rome were not immune to the occasional escape, including the sensational breakout of Giuseppe Pignata in 1693.[37]

Matters in the Holy Office had not changed at all twenty-five years later. In 1698 Inquisitor Giacinto Messerano (1698-1703) presented the usual complaints on the lack of 'safe and decent prisons'. The cells were in such a critical condition that one prisoner, the Venetian Pietro Liccini,

managed to dig his way through the wall for eight times in less than a year.[38] This feat was possible since the prison walls had not been originally constructed to serve for that purpose and, besides being fragile, they allowed easy communication with people outside. Notwithstanding numerous hasty repairs, these walls had become completely useless.[39] Messerano was finally instructed to draw up a plan for the construction of new prison cells,[40] and Rome at last agreed to vote 600 *scudi* for the project.[41] Twelve new prison cells were built on three different levels on top of each other, with an interconnected drainage system that provided sanitary facilities in the cells for the prisoners. The latter is an important indication that the Inquisition was also concerned about the actual physical comforts of the prisoners, and not solely with their spiritual wellbeing. Six of the seven surviving cells probably built by Messerano measure 2.8 x 2.3 metres, while the remaining one measures 4.8 x 4.8 metres. The wall touching the street outside was built anew and strengthened. A courtyard with a well in its centre was also created. This was made possible by digging through the bedrock. The problem of communicability with persons outside was partly solved by building a corridor through the prisons, thus eliminating all contact with the outside world, at least for some of the cells. The exit from the prison complex led to an 'extremely handy' flight of stairs through which prisoners could be led to the tribunal without them having to pass through the main staircase of the palace.[42] This new section of the prison was connected to the section built by Gori Pannellini in the 1640s by means of a wide arched

door, while a narrow flight of stairs led straight to the tribunal room.

Although far from solving all problems, Messerano's was the last known major intervention that finally provided the building with a prison complex worthy of its name. In fact no other major developments concerning the prisons seem to have been carried out during the eighteenth century. The changes would perhaps be better defined as cosmetic touches rather than real structural modifications, since the framework had been definitely set first by Gori Pannellini and then by Messerano.

Shortly afterwards, for instance, Inquisitor Giorgio Spinola (1703-06) modified part of the prison complex to separate the prisoners of the Holy Office from those of the *Reverenda Fabbrica*. This had not been possible previously, since the cells only allowed for the separation of male from female prisoners without taking into consideration which tribunal had imprisoned them, thus putting in jeopardy the secrecy of the Inquisition proceedings.

Spinola also obtained permission from the *Suprema* in Rome to spend a total of 132 *scudi* to transform one of the cells into a chapel for the exclusive use of the prisoners.[43] In 1705 the *depositario* of the *Reverenda Fabbrica*, Stanislao Xara, was paid 120 *scudi* for half of the sum spent in building the prisoners' chapel and other necessary repairs in the prisons.[44] This was another step forward towards increased security because previously prisoners had to be escorted out of the palace by the prison warden in order to carry out part of their sentence, such as hearing Mass,[45] thus providing another possibility of escape. It is possible that the chapel was one of the cells in front of the tribunal room, which still shows traces of holy figures painted on its walls.

Another minor intervention in the prisons took place in 1733 when, during other major structural works being carried out by Inquisitor Giovanni Francesco Stoppani (1731-35), one of the retaining walls of the main staircase collapsed onto some cells, which therefore had to be hastily repaired.[46]

Figures of saints in one of the cells which could have been used as a chapel

FINANCING THE PRISONERS

The structure of the cells was only part of the problem related to the management of the prison complex. Most important of all were the prisoners themselves, who had to be taken care of and provided with their basic needs. The sum needed for the food and other necessities of the prisoners was, in fact, one of the major recurrent expenses incurred by the tribunal, whose financial position was nearly always in the red and could ill afford such expenses.

In reality prisoners who could afford it had to pay for their own expenses while in prison, as was common practice in contemporary prison institutions.[47] In 1597, for instance, the Dominican fathers of Rabat paid the expenses the Holy Office had incurred to keep one of their brethren in gaol.[48] In 1606 Inquisitor

Diotallevi was instructed to force the *Monaci Cassinesi* to pay for the food and clothes of one of their members, Don Adeodato da Monreale, who had been imprisoned for apostasy.[49] The normal rate to be paid for the food was three *scudi* a month.[50] The expenses, however, could be particularly high if the prisoner had health-related problems. Such was the case of Fr Carlo Girolamo di Pavia, who fortunately could afford the 23 *scudi* 6 *tarì* 10 *grani* which the tribunal had paid for him during his arrest from February to June 1774.[51] However, most of the prisoners did not have enough money to pay for their food or other necessities. The tribunal, consequently, had to fork out the money for their daily rations, since it was standard procedure that 'when the accused does not have the means to

One of the solitary cells built by Gori Pannellini in the 1640s, later demolished

18

pay for his food, the tribunal is obliged to provide for him'.[52] Such was the case of Giuseppe d'Attard, whose *alimenti* from December 1715 to May 1716 cost 10 *scudi*, and the bill had to be footed by the tribunal.[53] In similar cases the tribunal would have been doing the charitable work which confraternities or other compassionate visitors usually did in public prisons.[54]

In actual fact there was another way to overcome such economic difficulties. In 1618 Inquisitor Fabio della Lagonessa (1614-19) found it expedient to sentence Aloisio de Gusman to pay 40 *scudi* to the auditor of the Inquisition 'for the food of the poor prisoners', since the Holy Office found it difficult to raise its own funds for this purpose.[55] It was, in fact, one of the established 'principles' of the Holy Office that fines collected had to be used for the upkeep of the prisons and the necessities of the prisoners. In such cases, however, it had to be pointed out in the sentence that the money was to be used for that end only, and it had to be deposited directly into the hands of the *depositario* and it could not be used for any other purpose.[56]

However, resorting to financial sentences was rarely used after the sixteenth century since the official policy of the Holy Congregation of Rome was not to appear as being interested in financial gains or material wealth.[57] After all, as the instruction manual used by the inquisitors made clear, the Holy Office had been instituted to safeguard the spiritual health of Catholicism. It therefore had to remain 'distant from casting any shadow of conflict of interest, and therefore of giving fiscal penalties, if not exceptionally'.[58] By the early seventeenth century, in fact, the practice of expropriation and of fiscal penalties, though not completely eliminated, had dwindled to a minimum in all Roman Inquisition Tribunals across Europe,[59] including Malta.

This policy put more pressure on the inquisitors for the management of the prison complex. In 1638 Inquisitor Fabio Chigi protested that he barely had enough money to pay for the expenses of the prisoners of the Holy Office.[60] In actual fact the expense for prisoners was not a small one. For the five years between 1658 and 1663, for instance, the sum amounted to 380 *scudi*,[61] while in the two years from 1676 to 1678 the tribunal incurred more than 139 *scudi* in expenses.[62] In 1688 the Holy Office was in such financial dire straits that it could not afford to pay for the food of the prisoners, and the *Reverenda Fabbrica* came to the rescue by providing 50 *scudi* usually distributed in pious causes. In the late 1760s, Inquisitor Giovanni Mancinforte (1767-71) calculated that the tribunal spent around 130 *scudi* annually for the maintenance of the prisons and the needs of the prisoners. This burden was too heavy for the Holy Office since it had a deficit of over 1,000 *scudi*.[63]

The flight of stairs leading from the prisons to the Tribunal Room

THE PRISON WARDEN

Another potential source of trouble in the management of the prison complex was the person who was supposedly responsible for its administration: the prison warden, who was one of the officials of the tribunal.

The prison warden was responsible for the safety and the security of the prisons and the well-being of the prisoners. An essential part of his job was to visit the prisoners at least every morning and evening to take them food and water rations. It was not his duty to visit the prisons during the night, but the inquisitor could order him to do spot checks every now and then to look through the *fenestrella* in every prison door to see that everything was proceeding well. Everything the prisoners received from outside had to be checked by him, or sometimes by other ministers of the tribunal. He had to open the door of the cell to let them out for their *cose necessarie* when they did not have the facility in their own cell. Sometimes he even bought some things for them with the money they gave him, or else accompanied them out of the palace to carry out part of their sentence, such as hearing Mass. It was also the gaoler's responsibility to open and close the main door of the palace every morning and evening, the keys of which he kept together with those of the cells.[64] In the 1650s the gaoler Thomaso Seychel was apparently also responsible for the general works being carried out in the garden of the palace.[65] It was also not unusual for the prison warden to have an assistant. In this respect, the prison of the Holy Office did not compare well with the *Gran Prigione* in

Valletta, near the Holy Infirmary. The latter came under the responsibility of the *prodomo*, who was the governor of the prisons and could decide upon the punishment. The *prodomo* had to manage the *agozzini*, responsible for distributing the prisoners in work gangs, and the *carcerieri*, who acted as guards.[66] It should be remembered however that there were many more inmates in the slaves' prison than in the prisons of the Inquisition.

In the early seventeenth century, when the cells were still spread all over the palace, the gaoler's room lay next to the main entrance of the palace. In 1631, besides storing a number of mattresses and blankets that he distributed among the prisoners, the gaoler also took care of the torture instruments: a rope and the *cavalletto*. The *manetti di ferro* and a pair of dice used by the prisoners to gamble to while away the time were also kept in his room.[67] By the second half of the seventeenth century, his room was moved to the first floor, more towards the centre of the palace, and much nearer to the new location of the prisons and to the 'old' section constructed by Gori Pannellini. By 1700, however, during some other structural works, his 'office' was once again moved downstairs to the room around which there is the 'secret' flight of stairs which leads straight from the prisons to the chancery and the tribunal room.[68]

In the late sixteenth century the gaoler earned 24 *scudi* annually.[69] Later on he started receiving 30 *scudi*. From 1668 on his salary was increased to 45 *scudi*,[70] while by 1735 it had risen to 54 *scudi*.[71] In actual fact the warden ranked fifth in the salary scale

of the ministers of the Inquisition. First came the inquisitor with 100 *scudi* monthly, then the chancellor (84 *scudi* yearly), the captain (48 *scudi* yearly), and then the assessor and *promotor fiscale* (47 *scudi* yearly). Only the cursors and the *depositario* earned less than the gaoler with 30 *scudi* annually. Both the gaoler and the cursors received a customary tip from the inquisitor every Christmas.[72] This fifth position, however, differed only by three *scudi* from the third place. Considering that the warden did not need to be literate or have any particular skill, his salary compared very well with those of the other ministers of the tribunal, and reflected the importance of his job in (officially) securing secrecy and the prison's security.

As an official of the Holy Office the warden had to lead an exemplary life and carry out his job dutifully. One gaoler who was recommended for his dedication was Zaro Xerri who had performed so well that, on his retirement in 1675, he was awarded a pension of half his annual salary by Inquisitor Ranuccio Pallavicino.[73] The same happened to Pietro Muscat in 1758 who, however, continued to receive his full pay.[74]

Other gaolers, however, were far from exemplary and added to the problems of the administration of the prisons, instead of helping solve them.

In 1593 the gaoler Theodoro Xuereb was accused of sorcery in front of the tribunal. Although there was not enough proof to condemn him, he was imprisoned for two years by Inquisitor Giovanni Ludovico dell'Armi. Xuereb was very disappointed at the way he had been treated by his 'employer' and he eagerly awaited the chance of getting even with dell'Armi. As soon as the latter left the island, Xuereb revealed to his successor, Inquisitor Innocenzo del Bufalo de' Cancellieri (1595-98), that dell'Armi had indulged in frequent illicit relations with a certain Lorenza Crispo. However, there was not enough proof to substantiate his claims and the indictment remained a dead letter.[75]

In the 1630s, notwithstanding the warnings by Inquisitor Martino Alfieri (1631-34) to pay maximum attention, warden Giuseppe Galdes kept indulging in lengthy discussions with the prisoners or even entering the cells to drink wine and play cards or with dice on the *tavoliero da giocare*. Galdes had originally been employed as a baker by Inquisitor Fabrizio Verallo (1600-05). In 1625, however, presumably because of his age, he was appointed warden. On one occasion, during the carnival revelries of 1633, when Galdes was seventy-three years old, five prisoners took advantage of his *laissez faire* attitude to escape through the main door, which he had left distractedly open while he was sewing in his room. Mami Rais and Gio. Battista Cagliares, using a nail, opened a padlock which they had previously greased with oil so that it would not make noise when being forced open. They climbed on to the roof of the palace with the help of two coats which they tied together, descended into another internal courtyard, and set free another three prisoners, Gioanne, Costantino and Ahmed, from another cell. Ahmed had been imprisoned that same day. The five of them went to the open countryside, changing their shelters every night and eating whatever they could find in the fields. They proceeded slowly towards the sea in search of a boat on which to sail away from Malta, but, after four days on the

The demolished solitary cells of Gori Pannellini

run, they were captured 'by the people' in the whereabouts of Corradino and brought back to the palace.[76] Alfieri informed his superiors in Rome about the escape, and he was instructed to put the escapees back in prison without 'further punishments'.[77] Galdes was imprisoned during the proceedings of the case.

Another warden who ended in trouble was Carlo Vella. In 1670 he was dismissed from his job after a series of blunders, the most serious certainly being the stabbing of Antonio Ravè, to whom Vella was in debt. He was also imprisoned for having revealed confidential information which, as an officer of the Inquisition, he was bound to keep secret by an oath.[78] Another warden, Andrea Mifsud was deemed responsible for the escape of a prisoner and was dismissed in 1685 during the tenure of office of Inquisitor Innico Caracciolo (1683-86).[79]

In 1717 the Holy Congregation thought it necessary to inform all inquisitors that the prison warden of the Holy Office of Spoleto, the Dominican friar Egidio Giorgi, had been sentenced to seven years' imprisonment for breaking the oath of secrecy.[80] It was thought that such warnings would act as a deterrent. Still another such case occurred in Malta in the 1740s, when the warden Pietro di Cristoforo and his assistant Giovanbattista Lombardini were imprisoned for the same infringement. After they had spent about a year in prison, Inquisitor Paolo Passionei (1743-54) received instructions from Rome to free them since the time they had spent in prison was enough punishment. However, from then onwards, upon accepting his duties, each warden was warned that he would be imprisoned for five years if he did not carry out his job dutifully. Lombardini asked to be re-appointed warden but his plea was ignored by the inquisitor who appointed Carlo Genovesi in his stead.[81] Even Inquisitor Giovanni Francesco Stoppani found it expedient to change his warden in 1731 since he discovered that 'he was not reliable enough on his job'. However, he decided to award him an allowance for his forty years of service to the tribunal 'to be able to survive in his extreme poverty'.[82]

Other gaolers abused outrightly of their position of authority *vis-à-vis* the prisoners. In 1622, for instance, Antonio Bellia asked a Muslim slave to hand him his money to keep it in a safe place for him. However, when the prisoner wanted his money back, he was told that it was not possible since it had been spent long before.[83] A more serious abuse occurred in 1705 when the *carceriero* Lazzaro Seichel was found guilty of having had sexual relations with a female prisoner and of having revealed confidential information, for which abuses he was condemned for five years on the galleys.[84] Another similar case took place in 1756, when warden Pietro Muscat was granted special leave to go and have dinner with his family in Valletta. His assistant, Giovanni di Lorenzo, took advantage of his absence and sexually abused Antonia Habela in the bed of her cell.[85]

The relatively frequent escapes, as well as the 'non consonant' behaviour which the prisons' precarious condition allowed the prisoners to indulge in, were a constant source of trouble and embarrassment to the Inquisition. In 1702, the cardinals of the Holy Congregation in Rome warned and reminded all inquisitors to visit the prisons frequently to ensure that no abuses were taking place. They also had to ensure that the wardens knew their duties perfectly well and that they were not to take any personal initiative as regards the prisoners or their sentences without previously consulting them.[86]

However, cases of abuse or escapes continued. In 1712 Giuseppe Franciscotti was left free to roam in the prison complex and escaped through the main door towards midday. Fortunately the inquisitor's cook was quick-witted enough to realize what was happening, ran after him, and caught him behind the Dominican church a few metres away from the palace.[87]

On 4 July 1725 Giovanni Maria Zammit, known as *Ciamano* from Mqabba, was imprisoned at the Holy Office. Twenty-six days later, on 30 July, he took advantage of the distraction of Vincentio Mendus who had been the gaoler for twelve years since 1713. As Mendus was drawing water from the well in the courtyard, Zammit sneaked out of his cell, which had not been locked, opened the main door (which the gaoler had left open), and locked the warden inside. He then rushed out of the palace and managed to get out of Vittoriosa disguised as a beggar. He roamed in the countryside for one month, managing to evade all attempts at his capture, until he was caught by officials of the civil courts on 31 August. However, he managed to escape once more from the palace on 14 September when he forced open the door of his cell. He waited for the warden to come and distribute the daily evening rations at 6 p.m. and, while Mendus was busy on his job, *Ciamano* rushed out of his cell and again locked the warden inside by closing the main prison door after him. He ran out of Vittoriosa, walked to Zabbar, and proceeded to Siggiewi. He finally sought refuge in the parish church of Mqabba, from where he asked to be accompanied back to the Holy Office by Inquisition officials after seven days, on 20 September.[88]

PRISON SENTENCES

Inquisitorial prisons had a double function. They were not only used for confinement as a punishment after a case had been concluded and a sentence given for unorthodox behaviour (*ad poenam*). Imprisonment also included temporary custodial detention of the accused pending trial until the investigation was complete and enough proof could be collected to commence proceedings (*ad custodiam*). Such prisoners were not told who had accused them or what they were being accused of, although sometimes they had a very precise idea of who had denounced them and for what offence. Undoubtedly custodial detention was also an effective way to enfeeble the resistance of the accused.

The prison complex was divided in two sections: those *ad poenam* were detained in the *prigioni secrete*, while those *ad custodiam* were kept in the *prigioni pubbliche*. In both cases, prisons had (officially) to guarantee the complete isolation of the accused so that he could concentrate on himself and his actions and thus become aware of his misconduct and

repent through a combination of discipline, correction, and mercy.[89] The aim was not merely to punish, but to provide conditions under which penitence would most likely take place. Isolation was meant to result in meditation, contrition, and, ultimately, salvation, much like the monastics of the early Church. In this sense, although the concept of isolation was not totally alien in early modern Europe, the Inquisition was a precursor of what was to occur in the nineteenth century, when isolation became an integral part of imprisonment thought.[90] The Church also went another step farther than civil law, for which imprisonment had a solely preventive function with no attempt being made at rehabilitation. It brought what was until then monastic imprisonment into the world of lay criminal justice, where prisons were more often than not communal rooms for groups of prisoners, rather than individual cells. Moreover, following the precepts of Roman law, imprisonment was used for confinement, not for punishment.[91] The function of

The warning above the main entrance of the prisons: *Once you have been admonished, teach justice and do not fear anyone*

inquisitorial prisons was, however, basically a penitential one aiming at spiritual redemption and rehabilitation. This concept is also made clear by the plaque on the door leading to the prison complex at the palace: *Discite iustitiam moniti et non temnere numen* (Once you have been admonished, teach justice and do not fear anyone).

The Holy Office apparently distinguished between those who were being detained temporarily and those who had received a specific prison sentence, reserving the 'worst' prison cells (the *secrete*) for the latter. A side note to a plan of the palace of around 1600 in fact specifies that three cells at ground-floor level 'are more to be used for punishment rather than for custody since, having no light, they are inhabitable'.

A sincere effort was thus made to separate the two types of prisoners. Luca Damato, suspected of false testimony, was detained *ad custodiam* but was found dead in his cell in 1744 before he had been interrogated.[92] On another occasion, in 1706 the slave Giuseppe Hasciac became seriously ill after four months in prison because the 'public' cell in which he was confined was too damp. Inquisitor Spinola, however, could not put him in another cell 'without locking him in the secret prisons', for which he did not 'qualify', and therefore he sent him back home to his owner.[93]

A prison sentence was relatively frequent, although it was usually of short duration. We still lack accurate statistics of the persons who were imprisoned by the Inquisition in Malta. However, although sentences varied from inquisitor to inquisitor, generally it seems that the prisons were used less and less as the Inquisition gradually decreased in importance during the eighteenth century. From a manuscript entitled 'Carcerazioni 1757-1798' held in a private collection, it would appear that no one was imprisoned at the palace between 1774 and 1777. Five persons were arrested in 1778, only to be followed by another 15 long years of inactivity until 1793. This list, which most probably included the 'criminal' as well as the 'civil' prisoners and the prisoners of the *Reverenda Fabbrica*, does not agree with a recently-published index,[94] but the main trends are somewhat similar.

The majority of those incarcerated were imprisoned more for the purpose of custody during trial rather than as a punishment for a proven crime. Most of them would eventually be found innocent and immediately released, thus showing the Holy Office's preoccupation with delivering a just sentence and its readiness to admit that it had arrested an innocent person to the detriment of his reputation.[95] Many served only a few days in prison. In 1794 Salvatore Cauchi from Zebbug was imprisoned for one day (1 March) for showing contempt towards Church dignitaries.[96] Others were acquitted immediately after their sentence, the time that they had spent in prison being deemed to have been an adequate punishment. Few served a very long prison sentence, and such sentences were generally cut short. In 1632, for instance, the two Greeks Gioanne and Costantino, accused of apostasy to Islam, were not sent to the galleys simply because they were 'disabled'. Officially, therefore, they were to be imprisoned for life and for five years respectively. Yet Gioanne was freed after three years, while Costantino was set free after a year and five months, notwithstanding the fact that they had attempted to escape from the prisons.[97] On another occasion, in 1675, after a long imprisonment, the Holy Congregation preferred to free the troublesome Don Matteo Barlotti rather than keep him imprisoned at the palace.[98]

The general leniency in prison sentences, however, besides that of real concern for the prisoners and the expenses that they incurred to the tribunal, is also an indication that the Inquisition possessed very little space in its prisons. On one occasion during the 1630s, Inquisitor Chigi had to slow down the sentencing process since the cells were so full that they could not host other prisoners.[99] This fact, which could be read between the lines on many occasions, emerges clearly in two sentences of 1639, when Claudio Simonet and Nicolo de Polo were both condemned to 'perpetual imprisonment' by Inquisitor Pannellini. After a few days, however, they were sent to row on the galleys 'since there is no place available at the Inquisition's prisons'.[100]

Where possible, therefore, the tribunal tried to kill two birds with one stone and free itself from the burden and responsibility of prisoners by liberating them, and thus 'not burdening the Holy Tribunal with further expenses'.[101] In July 1718 Inquisitor Pallavicino urged the Holy Congregation to decide what was to be done with the neophyte slave Fathalla, who had been imprisoned since October 1716. The officials of the tribunal were eager to liberate him to free them from the 'burden of such an imprisonment, which is an embarrassment'.[102] On other occasions prison sentences were changed to monastic imprisonment, house arrest, or confinement to a geographical area such as a particular

An inquisitorial sentence of 1639

town or village or the whole island. Thus, the slave Mahometto was confined to the slaves' prison;[103] Margarita Curt could not leave her house;[104] and Giovanni Pietro Cristodulus was transferred to the Capuchin convent in Rabat, Gozo.[105] In other cases Minichella Pulis had to confine herself to Valletta and the Three Cities,[106] while Giacomo di Matteo could not leave Malta for two years.[107] Such sentences were given especially if prisoners had behaved well and had showed signs of

Detailed records allow us to look into the past

forced labour on the galleys. Blasio Visei, a Genoese *buonavoglia* accused of false testimony, was sentenced to row on the galleys of the Order for two years;[111] the slave Soliman for five years;[112] and Gio. Antonio for ten years.[113] For the great majority of those who remained imprisoned at the palace, however, life was not as desperate as it was in most secular prisons of the time. To take the Order of St John as an example, knights were frequently sent to the *guva*, an underground pit or well, for lengthy stretches of time not only for serious crimes such as murder, but also for other offences such as assault, duels, blasphemy, breaking their vow of chastity, and even misbehaviour in church. Confinement in such a pit, from where escape was practically impossible, could even be accompanied by optional extras such as flogging.[114] Even conditions in the slaves' prison in Valletta were rather abominable, being described as squalid and normally overcrowded with unbearable air. The whole prison was just a large dormitory capable of hosting up to 900 inmates, divided according to age, with each prisoner having a small chest for personal items and rough bedding.[115] In the latter case, however, conditions were certainly not as desperate as in London's Newgate, which was synonymous with misery, despair, wickedness, squalor, and death, and where prisoners endured outrageous hardships, were brutalized, robbed, and starved.[116] In contemporary civil prisons, women and children were put together with adult criminals in cells with no beds or sewers. This usually led to a high percentage of death from typhus. Indeed many considered themselves lucky to come out of detention alive.[117]

repentance. In 1635 Inquisitor Chigi obtained permission to free Michele Signet because he had made great progress in the Catholic religion, even if he had to keep Malta as his prison for the time being.[108] Others were liberated because they had urgent impending work which could not wait, such as having to look after one's family or business, or keeping up with work at the fields or at sea.[109]

A very significant case reflecting the general attitude of the Holy Office towards imprisonment occurred in 1618, when Sulpitia de Lango was condemned to eight years' imprisonment for sorcery. After two years, however, she was released since she could not withstand incarceration and she had behaved like a good Catholic while imprisoned. A short while later she was given permission to move around within Valletta and in 1623 her confinement was extended to the whole of Malta.[110]

Others were not so fortunate, and their 'alternative' prison consisted of

PRISON LIFE AND CONDITIONS

Although deprivation of one's freedom was certainly not a pleasant experience, what might today appear as being incredibly harsh was not necessarily considered so by early modern standards. The strong emphasis on imprisonment as a very important part in inquisitorial procedure and its frequent use by inquisitors had a very important consequence. It increased officials' awareness of prison conditions, with the result that from the fourteenth century on, inquisitorial prisons were 'probably the best maintained prisons in Europe'.[118] Contrary to popular opinion, the conditions reserved for the prisoners of the Holy Office were certainly not the worst that could be experienced in early modern times, especially when one considers that chaining and beating of inmates were common practices throughout Europe until the end of the *Ancien Regime*.[119] It was common knowledge that the prisons of the Inquisition were less harsh and followed a more humane policy than civil or ecclesiastical prisons.[120]

Notwithstanding official regulations and concerns about secrecy, the 'prisoners of conscience' of the Holy Office could communicate with each other. This did not occur only when cells hosted more than one prisoner at a time because of lack of space. Prisoners, especially those detained in the *prigioni pubbliche*, could roam about in relative freedom within the prison and sometimes even within the ground floor of the palace, sweeping, cooking, or drawing water from the well.[121]

It was not contemporary practice to force prisoners to work since the utmost majority of them were there

Prison cell furniture: sleeping and sanitary facilities

only under custody and it was therefore considered immoral to abuse of them and force them to work.[122] Prisoners who carried out such general errands as described above, therefore, must have volunteered to do so, perhaps in exchange for some favour by the warden or as an excuse to leave their cells. Prisoners were usually left in complete idleness, something which sometimes led to despair. As a general rule prison sentences that included labour increased in popularity only in the eighteenth century. A fine example is the slaves' prison of Valletta, which was in reality a massive workhouse, providing the Order with the necessary muscle power to drive the galleys.[123] However, even the Inquisition seemed to have been a precursor in this aspect. Besides rowing on the galleys as mentioned above, the Inquisition also used other forms of 'social work'

as an alternative or concurrent with imprisonment. In the early 1650s Antonio Mercurio, a bigamist, and Mario Borg and Andrea Azzupard, two false witnesses, were sentenced to one day of forced labour *al fosso* every two weeks during the time they would spend in prison.[124] Women were even occasionally condemned to nurse the sick in hospital.[125]

Other types of 'freedom of movement' within the prisons were not lacking either. In 1633 the warden accompanied two prisoners, Gio. Battista Cagliares and the Greek Costantino, to a window on the first floor and to the main door of the palace respectively, 'to watch the carnival floats' during carnival. He also frequently sent them to the kitchen to bring him a plate of *maccheroni*.[126] A century later the warden Pietro di Cristoforo used to leave all doors of the civil and the

A breached cess-pit of a communal cell

criminal prison cells open so that prisoners could freely intermingle, both during the day as well as the night.[127] Apparently it was regarded normal for prisoners to consider the prison complex as 'their' territory where they could roam at will. In 1704 Inquisitor Giorgio Spinola thought it was 'improper that prisoners, left to roam about, even if the men separated from the women, had the facility to see and talk to each other'.[128] His efforts to secure confinement, however, proved fruitless, since the neophyte slave Giuseppe Hasciac was accused of having had 'a carnal relationship' with another slave, Teresa Piscopo, while both were imprisoned at the palace.[129] However this was a very rare exception and not the rule, as it was in fact in Newgate where illicit sex was available for any prisoner willing to pay for it. Male inmates paid the guards to allow their wives stay overnight or else paid for the services of prostitutes, and female prisoners freely engaged in sexual relations with their male counterparts in the hope of becoming pregnant so that they could 'plead their belly' and be pardoned.[130]

Nor were contacts with the outside world ruled out in the inquisitor's prison. This was first of all possible when the flimsy prison walls allowed communication with persons on the outside. Prisoners were also allowed to receive letters or other objects from outside after they had been checked by the warden or some other official. Pietro Beninschi was fortunate enough to be visited by relatives and friends,[131] while in the early 1660s, during the four years' imprisonment of the two British Quakers Sarah Cheevers and Katharine Evans, it was not unusual for them to talk with people who visited the palace.

Inquisitor Gerolamo Casanate even allowed them to have pen, paper, and ink to write to their relatives back home.[132]

On the other hand, food rations were not that abundant. In 1739 Inquisitor Ludovico Gualtiero Gualtieri reported to the *Suprema* that prisoners received only 15 *grani* worth of victuals daily: two loaves, some cheese and onions, without any soup or meat. He therefore asked that the tribunal be allowed to increase this sum to 20 *grani* daily for every inmate, and his suggestion was accepted.[133] Sometimes prisoners were given wine to drink as part of their daily food ration,[134] even though they certainly did not have the luxury of a wine tavern in the prisons, a comfort enjoyed by the inmates of the slaves' prison in Valletta only.[135] As a sort of compensation for this, prisoners of the Inquisition were permitted to buy their own food from outside (through the services of the warden, presumably for a small commission). They could also receive supplies from relatives and friends, including meat, fruit, and pasta, which they could eat in the company of their visitors.[136] While those who depended on the warden for their food presumably had more or less fixed eating times, those who received food from relatives or friends, or who purchased food from outside, apparently could eat whenever they wished. In fact there appears to have been no tight schedules, not even for eating, one of the main characteristics of modern 'total' institutions such as prisons, where the timing and sequence of activities is imposed organizationally from above.[137]

Other 'commodities' were not lacking either. Prisoners could make use of a candle during the night.[138] They had beds and straw mattresses

Water jugs found in one of the cess-pits

Grooves in the wall, possibly to hold candles

on which to sleep, which were regularly washed and repaired,[139] and blankets to cover themselves. Additional comforts were not excluded. In 1608 Betta Caloiro was allowed to put a heated brick under her bed to warm it up for the night.[140] From the bill of expenses of Girolamo di Pavia, it would also appear that washerwomen were employed to wash the clothes of prisoners, at least for those who could afford to pay for this service.[141]

General hygienic conditions were somewhat lacking, and Inquisitor Degli Oddi in 1657 listed it as one of the main problems of the cells. Some prisoners had toilet facilities in their cell, but others did not and therefore had to be accompanied out of their cell by the warden, who escorted them to the *luoghi necessari*. Some of the cells, especially those on ground-floor level, were (and still are) cold and humid. Sometimes detainees complained about the number of flies in their cells, which one of them interpreted as devils sent by God as a punishment![142] This obviously gave rise to health-related problems to some prisoners. In 1655, after two months in prison, sixty-year-old Don Giorgio Gauci complained that he was not feeling well. He was visited by Dr Michele Xeberras, who confirmed that Don Giorgio was 'troubled by colic pains' because of his damp cell. He therefore suggested that Don Giorgio should be transferred to another place that would be less deleterious to his health. This was duly done two days later, when Don Giorgio was sent to the house of a certain Don Torrensi in Valletta, which he had to consider as his prison.[143] Twenty years later, Dr Lorenzo Hasciac was called to check on Ismail Soltana, a seventy-

year-old Turkish slave. Hasciac found that Soltana was suffering from fever, had a dry tongue, and was refusing food. He was of the opinion that 'he must be sent to another place so that he could recover and free himself from the evident dangers in which he finds himself'.[144]

On another occasion, during the dreadful outbreak of plague which hit Malta in 1676, Inquisitor Pallavicino was seriously worried on the fate of two imprisoned apostates. He therefore left instructions to his successor Ercole Visconti that, should they develop the current malady, he should open a secret door so that 'it could be used by the infected doctors when they come to visit them. In this way they do not use the main door and you can therefore avoid it being barred by civil officials.'[145] One prisoner, in fact, became infected with plague and the sum of two *scudi* was paid for him to be carried away from the palace and for disinfecting the rest of the building.[146]

Every effort was made to keep the prisoners in the best possible conditions and to treat them kindly. Although this was done out of sincere motives, there was also an element of self-interest in it. Prisoners had the services of a doctor and a surgeon to check their state of health. In 1580 the Dominican friar Giuseppe Scicluna was found to be suffering from syphilis by doctors Francesco Saltalla, Camillo Russo, and Gregorio Mamo.[147] Prisoners' health was seriously taken care of, but this was a further expense for the tribunal which, besides paying for the doctors' visits, also had to foot the bill for the prescribed medicaments. In 1598 Maestro Camillo La Manda was paid five *scudi* for assisting 'in healing the sick prisoners',[148] and in 1715 the Holy Office spent no less than 32 *scudi* 'for the medication of a poor sick prisoner', and another five *scudi* 'paid to the herbalist Ignatio Cascin for the medicines bought from his pharmacy on behalf of the prisoners'.[149] It also made much sense, therefore, from the tribunal's point of view, to improve conditions and to keep prisoners in good health, in order to avoid paying for similar medical services.

One way for the Holy Office to relieve itself from such a burden was to allow sick prisoners to cure themselves outside the palace. One such instance occurred in 1588, when Dr Antonio Tramontana, the medical consultant of the Inquisition, certified that Giovanni Xara, an imprisoned Dominican friar, was suffering from fever. Inquisitor Bellardito allowed the friar to return to his convent to undergo the necessary treatment.[150] In some cases sick prisoners were even allowed assistance from outside the palace. In 1756 Antonia Abela was sick and had 'continuous indispositions'. Lorenza Calleja, after being sworn to secrecy, was allowed to visit her regularly throughout her stay in prison in order to assist her.[151]

On other occasions, however, it was not possible to send prisoners outside for medication, or let other persons cure them in prison, since they either had nowhere to go or no reliable relatives to whom they could be given in temporary custody. Such a case occurred in 1677, when Ismail, imprisoned for apostasy, complained of feeling unwell. He was visited by the doctor of the Holy Office, Lorenzo Hasciac, who confirmed that Ismail was suffering from high fever. Hasciac recommended that he should be transferred to another cell that would not be of detriment to his health.[152] The Holy Office had to foot the bill in such instances.

Understandably, being imprisoned in a religious 'penitential' prison, inmates of the Holy Office were also provided with all the necessary spiritual comforts. In 1608 Betta Caloiro could confess in her own cell.[153] Prisoners sentenced to be instructed in the doctrines of the Catholic Faith were taught catechism by an appointed priest in their cells, and detainees were allowed to stroll in the complex reciting the rosary.[154] Until the early eighteenth century it appears that, similarly to other inquisitorial prisons (such as the Spanish ones), inmates were not allowed to hear Mass, except those who had been sentenced to do so and who were therefore accompanied outside the palace by the warden.[155] In 1703-04, however, Inquisitor Spinola wished to transform one of the cells into a chapel to be used exclusively by the

A prison toilet

The prison walls are covered with graffiti, mainly featuring ships

prisoners. His suggestion was accepted by Rome so that 'prisoners are no longer deprived of the commodity and consolation of hearing Holy Mass'.[156] By 1771 there was even a 'parish priest', Don Gio. Batta Paris, to see to the spiritual health of the prisoners.[157]

All these activities, however, still left plenty of time at the disposal of the inmates who were illiterate in their absolute majority. Having nothing else to do but with an abundance of time to spare, therefore, most kept themselves busy by venting their creative energy and expressing their feelings by decorating the walls of their cells with all sorts of graffiti to while away the time, most probably with an iron nail or, possibly, with a coin. In this way, while remaining anonymous, they found a way to assert their identity even while in prison, and perpetuate their memory by leaving their imprint for posterity. The graffiti included drawings of ships

and other marine craft, religious motifs or emblems (crucifixes and Holy Host) and other symbols (eight-pointed cross of the Order, the sun and the moon), dates (1635, 1645, 1740, 1744, 1761), and various initials. Some scribbled some words in Italian, English, or Greek, or else quoted in Arabic from the Koran, while some others marked the passage of time and counted their days in prison with the help of rudimentary calendars scratched in stone, which normally took the form of vertical lines in close succession in a comb-like pattern.[158] Many graffiti are imbued with a sense of fatalism. A Muslim prisoner scribbled 'God helps the patient' on a wall, while the great number of crucifixes, besides indicating a certain religious aspect, presumably must also have symbolized suffering. Ship graffiti, on the other hand, most probably reflect the work of those who worked on them: sailors. Predictably they are a common theme

THE PRISON EXPERIENCE AT THE INQUISITOR'S PALACE

on a small island such as Malta where ships have played a fundamental role in everyday life since time immemorial. In fact they have been interpreted as representing existential problems faced by people who experienced or anticipated having to face serious predicaments at sea.[159]

Gambling was another very popular pastime, most often with the direct and enthusiastic involvement of the warden himself. A limestone dice was found among other artefacts during a recent excavation in one of the cells.[160] Some inmates preferred to sing. As Inquisitor Chigi remarked in 1634, 'the prisoners sometimes help me to sleep with their repeated chants',[161] sometimes with the accompaniment of a musical instrument.[162]

Apparently prisoners were allowed to bring private possessions with them and receive gifts. On one occasion, a search in a cell revealed, among other things, three mattresses, two coats, a broom, material to sew socks, two boxes of tobacco, a bowl, two pairs of shoes, two sacks full of different things, shirts, trousers, a jacket, a blanket, three jugs of water, and a lantern.[163] In 1633 Gio. Maria Cagliares even had a small pet monkey in his cell, which had to be cured by the doctor of the Inquisition since it had injured its hand.[164] After all even prisoners detained in the prisons of the headquarters of the Inquisition in Rome enjoyed a rather comfortable stay. They had a number of chairs and tables in their communal cells, together with pen and paper, brooms, candles, books, beds, mattresses, and blankets, and were also allowed to wear wigs and receive visits; they also ate relatively well.[165]

One prisoner declared that he passed the time 'eating, drinking, and playing dice in the inquisitor's prison'.[166] Don Pietro Paolo Callus affirmed that, during his time in prison, he 'had purchased good food,

Prisoners whiled away the time leaving their mark on the prison walls

enjoying himself with the company of the parish priest of Senglea, Don Fortunato Vella'.[167] It is clear that inmates were still far from receiving a quasi-patriarchal form of discipline that developed later in the nineteenth century.[168]

Others, however, did not find prison life so relaxing, and attempts at escape constituted their major nocturnal activity. Preparations for escape boosted morale. By keeping up their hopes that one day they would regain their freedom as a result of their efforts, prisoners somewhat made their situation tolerable. Indeed some prisoners were less equal than others: being considered dangerous or liable to escape, they had fetters or chains tied to their feet. One such was Ibraimo, a slave of the Order, who in 1780 was imprisoned at the discretion of the inquisitor with a chain tied to his feet.[169]

Pietro Licini, guilty of apostasy to Islam, was certainly one of the worst prisoners ever to be hosted in the cells of the Holy Office. Licini was always quarrelling with the warden; he banged his head against the wall and had to be hospitalized; and he managed to escape no less than eight times in 1697-98. On one occasion he did so by removing a stone from the wall overlooking the street and jumping down together with another inmate, the Frenchman Giacomo Gueiran. Both were captured a short while later in Vittoriosa. Licini was still near the palace since he could not walk properly because of the chains around his feet. Still there was no stopping him, and barely a month later Licini was again on the run. This time he prepared matters beforehand and he managed to cut the chains round his feet with one of the window's hinges. It took him eight nights' work to cut them after the warden's evening visit. He then removed a floor slab and lowered himself into the cell underneath, where his friend and accomplice Gueiran had already dug a hole in the wall with a piece of iron after three days' work. They then tied six socks together to form a rope and lowered themselves in the street. Licini was caught some days later, but Gueiran escaped on board a French ship.[170] This escape is clear evidence of how inmates could communicate with one another.

Others were not so fortunate or determined enough and sought other ways to alleviate their suffering. In 1701 Lelio Gasparini tried to commit suicide by putting lime in his soup, but was discovered and quickly taken to hospital.[171] In 1736 the Calvinist Giovanni Ducos also threatened to kill himself during an attack of desperation.[172] In 1686 the Greek Demetrio Palamida cut his throat with a piece of iron in a moment of despair, although it appears that he recovered.[173] Others were successful in their intents. In 1721 Antonio Ribas committed suicide,[174] while in 1735 it was recorded that the Muslim Demetrio 'hanged himself in the prison'.[175]

It would seem that these types of prisoners refused to accept the imposition of authority and the intrusion of other humans into their lives and personality. They wanted to reassert freedom and individuality in the context of control and regimentation. To compensate, therefore, they engaged in various types of retaliating behaviour: psychological withdrawal, violence, or attempts to escape.[176]

Other unfortunate accidents also occurred. In 1779 warden Aloysio Damato reported how inmate

Antonio Cremona, guilty of magical practices and of having furiously attacked the cursor of the tribunal, 'has become mad'. He found him practically naked on all fours in his cell with his food scattered on the floor. Dr Angelo Paci was immediately called to verify. In his opinion Cremona had become '*maniaco*' and had to be taken to the *Sacra Infermeria* as soon as possible to be cured.[177]

In 1608 warden Giuliano Fenech related to Inquisitor Della Corbara how, during his regular daybreak visit of the cells, he had found the octogenarian Betta Caloiro dead in a corner of her cell. When summoned, physician Nicola Cilia testified that Caloiro had died owing to old age and possibly because of tuberculosis.[178] Another similar incident took place in 1706, when the Muslim slave Sayd, accused of sorcery, was found dead in his bed in the morning of 2 December 1706 only one day after he had been brought there. The doctors certified that he had died of a 'heart stroke'.[179] On the other hand, the neophyte Paolo Agius died in hospital the day after he had been taken there.[180]

CONCLUSION

These unpleasant cases, however, were the exception rather than the rule. In reality, inquisitorial prisons very rarely had the necessary resources to guarantee the 'ideal' conditions of isolation that it theoretically set out for itself. And yet the Inquisition tribunal is burdened with the notoriety of cruelty, brutality, and harsh treatment. This was the direct consequence of the general rule of secrecy imposed by the Holy Office. On finally leaving prison, prisoners were obliged to take an oath not to

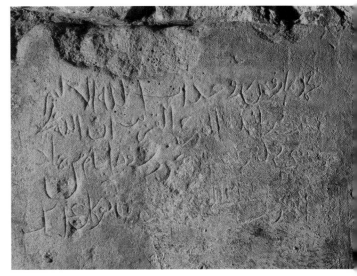

An extract from the Koran inscribed by an Arab prisoner

reveal anything they had seen, heard, or experienced in the cells. This secrecy gave rise to the most fantastic blood-curdling legends about what went on inside.[181]

Life in prison was bearable and prisoners enjoyed a limited freedom of movement. In the prisons there reigned a general atmosphere of informality and prisoners were relatively free to mingle with fellow inmates and visitors. Much like everywhere else in Europe, there was little sign of authority. Official efforts towards prisoner isolation, segregation by gender, and close surveillance of prisoners never really succeeded. It seems that there was not the right mentality yet for such concepts to be put in actual practice. Although the Inquisition certainly contributed towards the creation of a prison mentality by making frequent use of imprisonment as a punishment and to try and *reform* the prisoner, at least 'spiritually', it was not adequately equipped to carry out its mission to the full. Moreover, prisoners were a burden to the tribunal, especially financially. Rather than enjoy or congratulate themselves for having a full prison, inquisitors sought the means to get rid of the prisoners and were quite happy if the cells remained empty, for a number of reasons, first among which was finances.

Most probably this *laissez faire* attitude was a reflection of the novelty of the concept of imprisonment as a punishment. The sixteenth and seventeenth centuries were the formative and transitional period of incarceration. It was therefore difficult for wardens to adapt themselves to the necessary culture required for 'official' imprisonment. Nor were inquisitors really too worried about it either, as long as no escapes or great troubles which give rise to 'scandal' occurred.

Maybe it could be argued that inquisitorial prisons were the harbingers of the reform that took place in the nineteenth century, when reformation as distinct from mere punishment of the prisoner gradually became a more important theme. In the previous centuries, executions or punishment that took place in secret had no meaning. The fact that by the sixteenth century the Inquisition had *ad poenam* (imprisonment as punishment) cells, not simply *ad*

custodiam (temporary imprisonment while waiting for physical punishment) ones, was a very important breakthrough in imprisonment culture. The ideas of reform and cellular isolation in inquisitorial prisons were not reflected in secular prisons. Whereas in the civil penal mentality of the early modern period the prisoner was made to 'pay' for his misdeed through an often brutal public physical punishment, the Inquisition, by using imprisonment as a punishment, slowly shifted attention towards 'improving' and 'reconstructing' the personality of the accused to a point where he became again acceptable to society.[182] Obviously the Inquisition was more concerned with achieving this from the spiritual point of view. Although public physical punishment or humiliation was not eliminated, the frequent recourse to imprisonment as a punishment was a step in this direction, and the emphasis of the reformation of the prisoner 'left a strong imprint upon later thought and social theory'.[183]

NOTES

1 J.A. Sharpe, *Crime in early modern England 1550-1750* (London-New York, 1984), 181-2.
2 M. Foucault, *Discipline and punish. The birth of the prison* (Harmondsworth, 1979).
3 C. Fornili, *Delinquenti e carcerati a Roma alla metà del '600* (Rome, 1991), 72.
4 See P. Spierenburg, *The spectacle of suffering. Executions and the evolution of repression from a preindustrial metropolis to the European experience* (Cambridge, 1994).
5 Fornili, 74, 229.
6 See P. Spierenburg, *Prison experience. Disciplinary institutions and their inmates in early modern Europe* (Cambridge, 1991).
7 P. Spierenburg, 'The body and the state. Early modern Europe', in N. Morris and D. J. Rothman, ed., *The Oxford history of the prison. The practice of punishment in western society* (Oxford, 1985), 61.
8 See G. Parker, 'Some recent work on the Inquisition in Spain and Italy', *Journal of Modern*

History, liv, 3 (1982), 519-32.
9 For a general history of the palace see K. Gambin, *The Inquisitor's Palace*, Vittoriosa (Malta, 2003).
10 N. Johnston, *Forms of constraint. A history of prison architecture* (Illinois, 2000), 29-32.
11 Fornili, 75-6.
12 AIM, Proc. Crim., Prae IB, *Registrum introitus et exitus Sanctissimae Inquisitionis 1563-1635*, ff.37-v.
13 See AIM, *Computa 1658-1709*, ff. 62, 70, 106.
14 AIM, Corr.1, f. 205, Holy Congregation to Diotallevi, 10 September 1605.
15 Ibid., f. 285, Cardinal Arigoni to Della Corbara, 28 July 1607.
16 Ibid., Corr.2, f. 55, Cardinal Millino to Carbonese, 20 January 1610.
17 Ibid., f. 71, Cardinal Millino to Carbonese, 8 May 1610.
18 Ibid., Corr.3, f. 171, Cardinal Millino to Della Lagonessa, 21 September 1616.

19 Ibid., Corr.2, f. 79, Cardinal Millino to Tornielli, 25 June 1620.
20 Ibid., Corr.4, f.105, Cardinal Millino to Torello, 15 November 1621.
21 A. Bonnici, *Medieval and Roman Inquisition in Malta* (Malta, 1998), 264.
22 BAV, Chigi, A.I.3, f. 277, Chigi to Honorati, 23 February 1635; f.349, Chigi to Honorati, 17 July 1635; f.371, Chigi to Ugolini, 1 May 1638.
23 Ibid., A.III.57, f. 125, Gori Pannellini to Chigi, 30 November 1640.
24 Ibid., f. 124, 23 October 1640: 'more prison cells than prisoners'.
25 The three large cells (*pubbliche*) and the private apartments are still extant today and Gori Pannellini's name can be observed inscribed on the door lintels of the latter as well as on the entrance to 'his' prison section. The first two cells measure 2.8 x 5.8 metres, while the third one is 6.2 x 5.8 metres. It is not known when the remaining four cells, of which today only the doorways remain standing, were demolished, but most probably this occurred during the British military occupation of the palace (1800-1906) to make space for a 'racket court'. One of the three large cells was instead transformed into a wine cellar. From marks in the side wall which today forms part of the garden it is possible to arrive at an approximate measurement of the cells, which probably measured 3 x 3.8m.
26 AIM, Corr.10, f. 124, 10 February 1657, Cardinal Barberini to Degli Oddi.
27 Ibid., f. 200r-v, 14 December 1658; f.235, Cardinal Barberini to Casanate, 29 March 1659; Proc. Crim.70, case 3, f. 28v, Cardinal Barberini to Casanate, 15 February 1659.
28 AIM, Corr.12, f. 173v, Cardinal Barberini to Pallavicino, 26 March 1672.
29 Ibid., Corr.10, ff. 235-v, Cardinal Barberini to Casanate, 29 March 1659.
30 A. Bonnici, *Maltin u l-Inkiżizzjoni f'nofs is-seklu sbatax* (Malta, 1977), illustrations.
31 AIM, Corr.11, f.132, 26 January 1664, Cardinal Barberini to Marescotti.
32 Ibid., Corr.12, f.173-v, Holy Congregation to Pallavicino, 26 March 1672.
33 Ibid., ff. 232-v, Cardinal Barberini to Pallavicino, 6 May 1673.
34 Ibid., Corr.13, f. 74, Cardinal Barberini to Pallavicino, 30 March 1675.
35 Ibid., Corr.14, f. 162, Cardinal Cybo to Caracciolo, 31 March 1685.
36 G. Bonello, 'In and out of the Knight's prisons: 1530-1600', a six-part series in *The Sunday Times* [of Malta], 27 October – 1 December 2002.
37 P. Barrera, *Una fuga dalle prigioni del Sant'Uffizio (1693)* (Verona, 1934).
38 AIM, Corr.16, f. 67, f. 103, Cardinal Cybo to Messerano, 12 July and 8 November 1698.
39 Ibid., Corr.94, f. 3v, 9 August 1698; ff.9-v, Messerano to Holy Congregation, 25 October 1698.
40 Ibid., Corr.16, f. 103, Cardinal Cybo to Messerano, 8 November 1698.
41 Ibid., f. 108, Cardinal Cybo to Messerano, 6 December 1698.
42 Ibid., Corr.94, f. 26v, Messerano to Cardinal Cybo, 13 February 1700.
43 AIM, *Memorie* 5, ff. 31-v, Holy Congregation to Spinola, 27 October 1703; Corr.94, ff. 96v-97, Spinola to Marescotti, 6 September 1704.
44 AIM, *Computa 1658-1709*, f. 182v.
45 AIM, Proc. Crim.50A, case 135, f. 217v.
46 AIM, Corr.95, ff. 25v-26v, Stoppani to Holy Congregation, 24 July 1734. For the general project of Inquisitor Stoppani, see K. Gambin, 'Carapecchia's intervention at the Inquisitor's Palace 1733-34', *Malta Archaeological Review*, 4 (2000), 34-9.
47 H. Gross, *Rome in the age of enlightenment. The post-Tridentine syndrome and the ancien regime* (Cambridge, 1990), 224-6.
48 M. Fsadni, *Id-Dumnikani fir-Rabat u Birgu sa l-1620* (Malta, 1974), 222.
49 AIM, Corr.1, ff. 229, 277, Cardinal Arigoni to Diotallevi, 7 January 1606, 24 March 1607.
50 AIM, Proc., Prae 1B, f. 75v: [1580].
51 F. Ciappara, *Society and the Inquisition in early modern Malta* (Malta, 2001), 489-90.
52 AIM, Corr.30, f. 66, Holy Congregation to Salviati, 28 June 1755. See Ciappara, 488.
53 AIM, *Computa 1710-46*, f. 93.
54 D. Sella, *L'Italia del Seicento* (Rome-Bari, 2000), 171-2.
55 AIM, Proc. Crim., Vol.35A, f. 112v.
56 AIM, Corr.1, f. 241v, Cardinal Arigoni to Diotallevi, 20 May 1606; Ciappara, 480.
57 Ibid. 2, f. 71, Cardinal Millino to Carbonese, 8 May 1610.
58 AIM, *Miscellanea 2*, 79.
59 V. Lavenia, 'I beni dell'eretico, le entrate dell'inquisitore. Inquisizione romana e confisca, secc. XVI-XVII' in *L'Inquisizione e gli storici: Un cantiere aperto* (Rome, 1999).
60 BAV, Chigi, A.I.4, f.371, Chigi to Ugolini, 1 May 1638.
61 AIM, *Computa 1658-1709*, f. 8v.
62 Ibid., f. 70.
63 AIM, *Memorie 20*, f. 17.
64 AIM, Proc. Crim.50A, case 185, ff. 210v-35.
65 AIM, *Computa 1658-1709*, f. 9.
66 D. Borg-Muscat, 'Prison life in Malta in the 18th century. Valletta's Gran Prigione', *Storja 2001*, 47.
67 AIM, Proc. Civ., *Inventario 1631*, ff. 271r-v.
68 AIM, Corr.94, f. 27, Messerano to Holy Congregation, 13 February 1700.
69 AIM, Proc., Prae 1B, f. 63.
70 A. Bonnici, *Storja ta' l-Inkiżizzjoni ta' Malta*, II (Malta, 1992), 112.
71 AIM, *Computa 1710-46*, f. 319.
72 Ibid., *1658-1709*, ff.103-4.
73 Bonnici, *Storja ta' l-Inkiżizzjoni*, II, 149.
74 A. Bonnici, *Storja ta' l-Inkiżizzjoni ta' Malta*, III (Malta, 1994), 251.
75 A. Bonnici, *Storja ta' l-Inkiżizzjoni ta' Malta*, I (Malta, 1990), 136-7.
76 AIM, Proc. Crim.50A, case 185, ff.208-59v.
77 AIM, Corr.6, ff.37, 53, Cardinal Onofri to Alfieri, 27 August and 26 November 1633.
78 Bonnici, *Storja ta' l-Inkiżizzjoni*, II, 122-3.
79 AIM, Corr.14, f. 162, Cardinal Cybo to Caracciolo, 31 March 1685.
80 Ibid.21, f. 113, Holy Congregation to Pro-Inquisitor Napulone, 13 November 1717.
81 Bonnici, *Storja ta' l-Inkiżizzjoni*, III, 194-5.
82 AIM, Corr.94, ff. 282v-3, Stoppani to Holy Congregation, 13 October 1731.
83 Bonnici, *Storja ta' l-Inkiżizzjoni*, I, 208-9.
84 AIM, Corr.94, ff.108v, 120-v, Spinola to Marescotti, 7 March 1705, 9 January 1706.
85 AIM, Proc. Crim., Vol.125A, case 546, ff. 42-98v.
86 AIM, Corr.17, f.15, Cardinal Marescotti to Messerano, 19 March 1702.
87 Ciappara, 485.
88 M. Xuereb, 'Apostasy and the Inquisition in Malta 1720-1730' (BA Hons unpublished dissertation, University of Malta, 1997), 125. See AIM, Proc. Crim.109B, case 420, ff. 696-8.
89 A. Prosperi, *Tribunali della coscienza. Inquisitori, confessori, missionari* (Turin, 1996), 197.
90 Foucault, 237.
91 E. Peters, 'Prison before the prison', in N. Morris and D.J. Rothman, ed., *The Oxford history of the prison. The practice of punishment in western society* (Oxford, 1985), 32-43.
92 AIM, Corr.95, f. 164, Passionei to Holy Congregation, 5 April 1744.

93 Ibid., Corr.94, ff. 102-v, Spinola to Marescotti, 9
   January 1706.
94 Ciappara, 518-38.
95 Ibid., 467.
96 Ibid., 535.
97 AIM, Proc. Crim.54Bis, cases 5-6, ff. 31-121v.
98 AIM, Corr.13, f. 74, Cardinal Barberini to
   Pallavicino, 30 March 1675.
99 BAV, Chigi, A.I.3, f. 277, Chigi to Honorati, 23
   February 1635; f. 349, 17 July 1635.
100 AIM, Proc. Crim. 54Bis, case 7, f. 143; Proc.
   Crim.53A, case 364, ff. 814-21.
101 AIM, Corr.96, f.174; Ciappara, 478.
102 AIM, Corr.94, ff. 211v-2, Pallavicino to Holy
   Congregation, 9 July 1718.
103 AIM, Proc. Crim.51B, case 125, ff. 839-40.
104 Ibid., Proc. Crim.51A, case 82, f. 400v.
105 A. Camenzuli, 'Maltese society in perspective
   1771-1798' (Unpublished MA dissertation,
   University of Malta, 1999), 54.
106 AIM, Proc. Crim.53B, case 366, f. 964v.
107 Ibid., case 365, f. 907.
108 AIM, Corr.88, f. 356v, Barberini to Chigi, 13
   October 1635.
109 Ciappara, 478.
110 C. Cassar, Sex, magic and the periwinkle. A trial at
   the Malta Inquisition Tribunal in 1617 (Malta,
   2000), 28-9
111 AIM, Proc. Crim.80, case 66, ff. 436r-v.
112 Ibid., Proc. Crim.79, case 27, f. 274v.
113 Ibid., Proc. Crim.61, case 150, ff. 741-86.
114 Bonello, 'In and out of the Knight's prisons', parts
   3 and 4, 10 and 17 November 2002.
115 G. Wettinger, Slavery in the islands of Malta and
   Gozo ca. 1000-1800 (Malta, 2002), 86-95. See
   also Borg-Muscat, 43.
116 W.J. Sheehan, 'Finding solace in eighteenth-
   century Newgate', in Crime in England 1550-
   1800', J.S. Cockburn, ed., (London, 1977), 229-
   30.
117 Johnston, 28.
118 Peters, 31.
119 R. Jutte, Poverty and deviance in early modern
   Europe (Cambridge, 1994), 169.
120 See H. Kamen, The Spanish Inquisition. An
   historical revision (London, 1998), 184-7.
121 AIM, Proc. Crim.50A, case 185, f. 216v.
122 Fornili, 89.
123 Borg-Muscat, 44. Workhouses developed first in
   Holland and Germany in the sixteenth century.
   Johnston, 33.
124 AIM, Proc. Crim.62, case 206, ff. 369-413.
125 Bonnici, Inquisition, 173.
126 AIM, Proc. Crim.50A, case 185, ff.217, 224.
127 AIM, Corr.95, f.166v, Passionei to Holy
   Congregation, 3 May 1744. Ciappara, 492.
128 AIM, Corr.94, f.97, Spinola to Marescotti, 6
   September 1704.
129 Ibid., f. 108v, 120r-v, Spinola to Marescotti, 7
   March 1705, 9 January 1706; Corr.17, ff. 267,
   306, Marescotti to Spinola, 11 April 1705, 9
   January 1706.
130 Sheenan, 243-5.
131 AIM, Proc. Crim.79, case 27, f. 251.
132 S. Villani: Tremolanti e papisti. Missioni quacchere
   nell'Italia del seicento (Rome, 1996), 123.
133 Ciappara, 488.
134 AIM, Proc. Crim.133C, case 400, f. 1401.
135 Wettinger, 123.
136 AIM, Proc. Crim.50A, case 185, ff. 225-6.
137 S. Mennell, A. Murcott, and A.H. van Otterloo,
   The sociology of food. Eating, diet and culture
   (London, 1992), 113-4.
138 AIM, Proc. Prae 1B, f. 87: [1580] Oglio et candele
   date al carceriere per se et per carcerati... per lumi et
   oglio per li carcerati.
139 AIM, Conti, Computa 1603-1606, unpaginated
   loose papers: Pagliaricci per li carcerati; AIM,

Computa 1658-1709: f. 9, 31 July 1658: per lavare
   e conciare diversi matarazzi, f. 181v, 11 March
   1704: per una investa di matarazzo per servitio delli
   carceri.
140 C. Cassar, Witchcraft, sorcery and the Inquisition. A
   study of cultural values in early modern Malta,
   (Malta, 1996), 90.
141 Ciappara, 490.
142 AIM, Proc. Crim.71A, case 158, f. 256.
143 Ibid., Proc. Crim.68B, case 69, ff. 528, 533v.
144 Ibid., Proc. Crim.79, case 2, f. 150.
145 AIM, Memorie 1, f.74v.
146 AIM, Computa 1658-1709, ff.62r-v.
147 Fsadni, 215.
148 AIM Conti, Computa Sant' Officio 1598-1600,
   unpaginated loose papers.
149 AIM, Computa 1710-46, ff. 81v-2.
150 Fsadni, 223.
151 AIM, Proc. Crim.125A, case 546, f. 47.
152 Ibid., Proc. Crim.79, case 2, f. 150.
153 Cassar, Witchcraft, sorcery and the Inquisition, 90.
154 Ciappara, 490.
155 AIM, Proc. Crim.50A, case 185, f. 217v.
156 AIM, Memorie 5, ff.31-v, Holy Congregation to
   Spinola, 27 October 1703.
157 Bonnici, Storja ta' l-Inkizizzjoni, III, 365.
158 See L. Sciascià, Graffiti e disegni dei prigionieri
   dell'Inquisizione (Palermo, 1977).
159 J. Muscat, 'Ship graffiti – A comparative study',
   Journal of Mediterranean Studies, ix, 1 (1999), 76-
   7. See also J. Muscat and J. Cassar, 'The Gozo
   prisons graffiti', Melita Historica, xi, 3 (1994),
   241-73.
160 Annual Reports of Government Departments – 2000
   (Malta, 2001), 168.
161 BAV, Chigi, A.I.3, f. 240, Chigi to Mignanelli, 15
   November 1634.
162 AIM, Proc. Crim.50A, case 185, f.219v.
163 Ibid., ff. 219-20.
164 Ibid., f. 223v.
165 Barrera, passim.
166 AIM, Proc. Crim.50A, f. 212.
167 Ibid., Proc. Crim.120B, f. 572. Quoted by
   Ciappara, 487.
168 Spierenburg, 'The body and the state', 49. For
   the civil prisons of Malta, see E. Attard, Il-Habs.
   L-istorja tal-habsijiet f'Malta mill-1800 (Malta,
   2000), 127-49.
169 Ciappara, 534.
170 Ibid., 484-5.
171 AIM, Corr.94, f.40, Messerano to Holy
   Congregation, September 1701.
172 AIM, Corr.95, f.45, Durini to Holy
   Congregation, 4 June 1736.
173 Ciappara, 484.
174 AIM, Corr.22, f.138, Cardinal Giudice to Ruffo,
   27 September 1721.
175 Ibid., Corr.26, f.121, Cardinal Ottoboni to
   Durini, 2 July 1735.
176 J. M. Coggeshall, 'Prisons', in Encyclopedia of
   cultural anthropology, III, ed. D. Levinson and M.
   Ember (New York, 1996), 1032.
177 AIM, Proc. Crim.133C, case 400, ff. 1401-2.
178 C. Cassar, Witchcraft, sorcery and the Inquisition,
   89-92.
179 AIM, Corr.94, f. 122, Caracciolo to Cardinal
   Marescotti, 4 December 1706; Corr.18, f.21,
   Holy Congregation to Caracciolo, 29 January
   1707; Bonnici, Storja ta' l-Inkizizzjoni, II, 323.
180 AIM, Proc. Crim.130, f.71. Ciappara, 495.
181 Kamen, 186.
182 B. Lenman and G. Parker, 'The state, the
   community and the criminal law in early
   modern Europe', in Crime and the law. The social
   history of crime in western Europe since 1500,
   V.A.C. Gatrell, B. Lenman and G. Parker, eds.
   (London, 1980), 44.
183 Johnston, 27.

THE PRISON EXPERIENCE AT THE INQUISITOR'S PALACE